MY PIXIE DIXIE

based on a true story

—— *by* ——

NIZA P. SCHEAR

2014

dedicated to

OUR THREE BEAUTIFUL CHILDREN—
Ahmree, Kobi & Sofie.
We're all in the same boat whether the waters are calm or turbulent.
I love you.

♡ Love
Health
&
Blessings
Nya

For more information or to order copies contact the author at:
mypixiedixiebook@gmail.com

contents

CHAPTER ONE

In the same boat

BEING DRAGGED AROUND the lake for a walk with my mom wasn't my favorite thing to do, especially on a gloomy, chilly, spring day. I was waiting for summer, but the long winter and cool spring didn't keep Mom from wanting to walk around her favorite lake, dragging me with her. That was fine when I was a baby, because I slept in my stroller on these walks, but now I'm nine.

"One mile, fine. Two miles, okay, but more than three miles? No way! How on earth are we going to walk around this enormous lake?" I complained to myself.

At the lake, I'd rather just sit next to my favorite tree – the tree that is green like the shades of a dollar bill. About five feet up its trunk is a big hole.

My tree is near the window of the lakeside ice cream shop. Sitting where I can see the tree, as I lick an ice cream cone, always makes me happy. I'm not so happy when Mom takes me walking around the lake; she talks to everyone she sees, which makes the walks worse, taking even longer. Our lake is a favorite place for many people, and Mom seems to know them all.

"Sadie," she would say, "can you go for a walk with me today?" Well, I'm just a typical nine-year-old girl, if there is such a thing. I like to swim and to draw. I also want to find a good friend I can trust. I learned even younger that we all are searching for something.

I also became aware of how hard it is to let go of things – especially the things we are used to and the people and things we love. Even though my great grandma was 93 when she died, I still think about her and miss her a lot. She was a strong and capable woman! I never wanted to let my great grandma go, and neither did my mom.

My mom is lot of fun, but lately she has been struggling to feel capable and strong. Mom, with a lot of education, wanted to find work that would make her happy – work at which she'd really be good. But something seems to be holding her back. Mom is really good at walking around the lake and making friends, but she needed more than that for real happiness – and to pay the bills.

Mom dragged other people around the lake, too; she wasn't the only one struggling to find happiness there. Aunty Miri was looking for love – the butterfly-in-your-stomach kind of love, and also the kind that says you've found your best friend for life. A love where your feelings of loneliness float away. A love with whom you can raise children – and smile as your kids jump in gross, muddy puddles. And a love where you both would agree to drag your kids around the lake.

Then there is my Uncle Dan. He lives in New York. He had been married a long time, but was getting divorced and just wanted to have a happy connection with his children, who were 12, 15 and 18. Uncle Dan needed his kids. Uncle Dan was moving out of their home, and his kids were drifting away from him even as they still needed him. He was feeling very sad about the changes in his life, felt lonely all the time and was frightened. He felt like he was just treading water in his life. Uncle Dan wanted to let go of his troubles and find happiness, but couldn't find a way.

Zachary, my older brother, was waiting patiently to fulfill a dream. My dad? He wasn't sure what he was seeking to make him happy but he was searching anyway. And then, there is my favorite grandpa in the whole world. He's 81, runs around like he's 20, and is one smart guy. He's an electrician and plumber who can fix almost anything. He wants to be happy too, and he holds tight to all of us; his happiness is knowing we're okay. That's just how he is. I guess you could say that we were all in the same boat, searching and looking for happiness. But something was holding us all back and because we didn't know just what it was, it was hard to let it go.

In spring 2013, that began to change for some of us. We learned the magic of letting go.

CHAPTER TWO

Homeless

So on a cool Saturday afternoon, instead of walking around the lake, Mom decided to sit by the docks and watch the waves and the dark clouds. We sat next to the ice cream shop window by the docks. Lucky day for me – no walking around the enormous lake!

"Sadie, stay near!" Mom reminded me as I walked a few steps away and sat next to a man busy carving something. As Mom kept a close eye on me, I kept a close eye on the man. He was making a tiny sailboat. Carved on the boat was its name, Pixie Dixie, and also his signature. It had a feather for a sail.

"How much is a boat?" I asked. The man handed me his completed carved sailboat, so small it fit in the palm of my hand, and said in a quiet voice, "It's free!"

I ran over to my mom, carefully holding my new tiny sailboat, made from a thick piece of bark. "Mom, look at my little sailboat with a feather as the sail," I said with excitement. "The man over there with the black stocking cap gave it to me! He told me that there is a secret about this sailboat. I need to know the secret about this Pixie Dixie!"

"Sadie, remember stranger danger?" Mom said with a stern look. "Okay Mom," I replied. "I saw you watching us, and if you meet him, he won't be a stranger." I pointed to the table, where the man was carving once more, making another tiny sailboat. His

short white hair peeked through his black stocking cap, which had a white anchor embroidered on the front. His ears stuck out of his cap, and he looked like a big elf.

"Mom, come and meet the boatman," I said, excited to make a new friend. Hand in hand, Mom and I walked over and asked the boat maker if we could join him at the table. The boatman's face was like the color of a white cloud. He was clean shaven and his lips didn't break into a smile, but without looking up, he gave us a welcoming nod and we sat next to him at the picnic table. We started asking him questions.

"I was married once and then I was homeless," he told us in a quiet, calm voice. "I love making these little sailboats." In the brief moment that he looked up, we noticed that his eyes were bright blue, like the lake when it reflects the sky.

As he looked down and returned to carving, I stared at him. "That's weird," I thought. "He certainly doesn't look like someone who could be homeless."

"Can I pay you for this little boat?" Mom asked. He gently refused the couple of dollars my mom held out and said, "No. I'm okay now; I have what I need." He continued working, using his pocketknife to chip away layers of another piece of bark to make his next boat.

CHAPTER THREE

I've made Thousands

"Why do you name your boats 'Pixie Dixie?'" I asked. "I like the name," he said. "Some people believe a pixie is a small elf or fairy that likes to dance or wrestle outside with other little pixies through the night. They act like little kids, those pixies. I suppose they dance to jazzy Dixie music," he said. "I just like the name Pixie Dixie," he repeated, as if jazzy Dixieland music was playing in his ear.

The boatman looked over at me and handed me a pen. "Here, use this pen and add your own name and design to your boat," he said, still paying attention to the new boat he was carving. I secretly wished to use the pocket knife, but I could hear my grandma Clava's voice echoing in my ear, saying: "Oye, oye, oye, you are going to chop off your fingers," so I settled for the pen. "My very own Pixie Dixie!" I said to myself.

Mom, always inquisitive, asked: "What's the story behind these Pixie Dixies?" The boatman pointed to the water as I continued drawing my daisies onto my boat. "One day, many years ago, I was by the docks over there as the sun was going down, and a little girl with her grandpa came up to me and asked me what I was doing," he said. "The sun was setting and the moon was out. I told the little girl and her grandpa to keep an eye on the water and watch the stream of light from the moon as it reflected on the water. At that moment a tiny Pixie Dixie boat I made floated in the stream of the

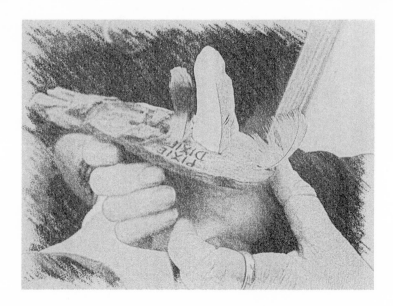

moonlight. We all kept a careful watch on Pixie Dixie as it floated to shore.

"The little girl ran over to the sandy beach and pulled the boat out." The boatman's words were so calm, like quiet water. "It made me happy to see her happy, so I just started making these little boats for others. I've made thousands since then. Each one different, each Pixie Dixie having its own journey," he said.

"Can I give you something for the boat?" my mom asked once again. "No, I just give them away," the boatman said. "I have what I need," he said softly, never taking his eyes off of his newly carved vessel as he added the final touch, his name.

The boatman handed my mom his completed Pixie Dixie, and placed it in the palm of her hand. The tiny sailboat had a feather as the sail. Mom held her tiny sailboat tight, as if she would never let it go. We each had a perfect little Pixie Dixie. Two tiny stones fitted into the bottom of each boat would keep them upright and balanced on the water. I could see my mom's eyes thinking as we held our Pixie Dixies.

CHAPTER FOUR

The Secret

As SHE READ the man's name on the top of her Pixie Dixie, Mom asked the boatman: "Should we call you Mark?"

"How about Captain Mark," he said, chuckling like a child.

"Mom, can we see the boatman again? Can we bring him something?" I asked.

She looked to Mark and asked what we could bring him. Captain Mark responded softly, with tranquil eyes. "A peanut butter, jelly and cucumber sandwich," he said in a serious voice. Mom cringed at the combination, but said, "Great! See you soon!"

I was pretty excited! "Peanut butter, jelly and cucumber sandwich?" That's kind of weird, I thought, but okay. And just before we left the boatman to finally get ice cream, at the ice cream shop window, by the lake, next to my favorite tree, the boatman kneeled down next to me and whispered the Pixie Dixie sailboat secret in my ear.

Even though it was one of those secrets you are supposed to share to make others happy, I wasn't ready to let the secret go – except to Mom. "Shhhhhh, don't tell anyone the secret yet, that the boat man told me, Mom," I whispered in a loud voice as I passed the secret on to her.

We called Grandpa to come spend time with us that dark afternoon. Grandma Clava stayed home to play on Facebook, and before

we knew it, Grandpa was at the table by the ice cream window by the lake. "Grandpa! Grandpa! Look at the sailboat I got from the man at the picnic table!" I shouted, showing him my very own Pixie Dixie.

"Let's put it in the water," Grandpa suggested.

"But I don't want to lose the new boat I got," I said, my voice filled with worry. Grandpa walked over to his car and opened his trunk. Everything you need is in that trunk. He has a box of tools, cables, wires and a long white string. Grandpa chose the string and wrapped it to the middle stone on the bottom of my Pixie Dixie sailboat. I threw my Pixie Dixie into the lake and we watched it bob on the bumpy waves as I held tight to the string. Then I pulled the string back and dragged my Pixie Dixie back to shore. I brought my Pixie Dixie sailboat home with me that day with the string still attached. That night, I stared at my Pixie Dixie as it rested on my cluttered dresser, my nightlight shining over it, and I thought about the boat secret, which was the secret hiding spot for the Pixie Dixie boats. My mom and I held onto the secret all night long.

CHAPTER FIVE

Tree Hole

But the very next day, Mom dragged me back to the lake for a walk, this time with my brother. Clever as are we, we grabbed our scooters. When we got to the part of the lake with the ice cream shop and the tree with a hole, I said: "Hey, Zachary, please lift me up, by my favorite tree, next to this heart-shaped tree hole, please!" He grabbed me by the waist and I stepped all over his legs as he lifted me up to peek in the tree hole. "Owwww!" he shouted. Without a clue of why he was lifting me, he did it anyway. "Oh nothing!" I said to myself, sulking. There was nothing in the tree hole!

The next day, my Aunty Miri was with us for the walk of the day. Being with beautiful Aunty Miri was like an adventure. Mom sat down in the huge wooden chair next to the ice cream window and closed her eyes to meditate and enjoy the warm sun.

"Aunty Miri, please come with me to that tree, next to the ice cream window, and check that tree hole with me, please!" I begged her. "Are you kidding?" she said. "I'm not putting my hand in that tree hole!" I stared at her, my hands on my hips and a smile on my face, and she gave in. Reluctant and scared she might be bitten by a squirrel hidden in the hole, reached in and felt something fuzzy. Aunty's heart skipped a beat, and she yanked her hand back out.

"Dig deeper, there's a surprise in there," I said. "Are you kidding?" she said again, making a face. But she did it, and this time,

Aunty Miri reached farther, past the soft fuzz. She closed her fingers and pulled her hand back; sitting in her palm was a Pixie Dixie sailboat ready to be cast away.

Aunty Miri was so surprised! "What is this sailboat about?" she asked. I was excited that Aunty Miri had found her own Pixie Dixie.

I could tell she began to love it. "This is how it works Aunty Miri. Like this: You close your eyes real tight, express your hopes, give good wishes to others while sending blessings for the lake on your Pixie Dixie and carefully let your tiny Pixie sailboat go on the water." Mom says that when you let things go, good things come back to you, especially if you are grateful for what you have. But I wasn't sure how that was supposed to work.

Aunty Miri had a hard time letting go of her Pixie Dixie, but we went to the dock by the shore and she closed her eyes and whispered. She whispered her hope of finding her true love, sent good wishes to others and said blessings for the lake over her Pixie Dixie as she carefully set her boat on the water. The stream of sunlight shined on her little boat.

"Look Aunty Miri, the light looks like dancing exclamation marks as it shines on the boat," I said. "It looks like flashes of light!" Then, as the sun kissed her little Pixie Dixie sailboat, it slowly went under the dock and out of sight. But her heart was happy. She hugged and kissed me, leaving a pink lipstick mark on my forehead.

CHAPTER SIX

Turbulent

WE SHARED OUR boat story with family and friends. Some of our friends also were struggling to find happiness. They were worried or afraid about things in their lives and had a hard time letting go of those fears. We told them that the magic of the boat was in its casting away.

"We need to make sure we share our hopes, putting good wishes and blessings on the Pixie Dixie sailboats, before we let them go," I said. "We want to make sure that the person who finds the boat gets a boatload of good wishes. That is the magic of Pixie Dixie."

I asked Captain Mark to make a boat as a birthday present for Uncle Dan, who was so troubled. I mailed it to him for his birthday, but instead of calming Uncle Dan, it frustrated him.

Tiny Pixie Dixie boats usually are sent sailing on the lake by the ice cream window and the secret tree. Uncle Dan tried to sail his little sailboat in the big ocean – the Atlantic to be exact. He told Mom that he'd piled on his hopes to connect with his children, sent many wishes for his children to be happy, blessed the ocean and launched his boat. But the tide was coming in, so the boat kept coming back. "We all want to belong, we all want to be wanted!" he yelled out loud to himself, wanting to connect with his children.

It's hard to let go when life is turbulent and the tide is working against you, I guess. I thought that maybe his hopes were too big for such a little boat – and so was the ocean.

CHAPTER SEVEN

Let Go

THE WEEKS WENT BY, and all too soon, summer vacation was coming to an end. Going back to school was harder than usual because the Pixie Dixie adventure had made me love the lake. Instead of feeling dragged around, I'd been asking Mom to take me there every day. "Can I drag you one last time to the lake?" I asked her. "I just want to sit next to my tree, by the ice cream shop window by the lake." I said.

Mom agreed, and we went with Dad and Zachary. We walked up to the tree, which I'd learned was a mighty oak that had lost a branch, leaving the heart-shaped hole. The leaves, which jutted out like little fingers, were turning yellow and brown. We checked the secret tree hole one last time, Dad carefully reaching in.

He brought out five little boats! We had a Pixie Dixie for each of us and one extra! We decided to put one back for someone else to find – someone who might need it more than we did. I reminded myself: Let go, and happiness will come back to me. Be grateful for what I have. I repeated that over and over in my head.

As we walked by the lake, holding hands, I looked back and saw a girl I'd known since kindergarten but hadn't taken the time to know well. She was eating an ice cream cone by my favorite tree. I ran toward her, pointed to the tree, whispered the Pixie Dixie hiding place secret in her ear and gave her my tiny Pixie Dixie sailboat.

Running back, I saw my brother close his eyes real tight as he expressed his hopes – he wants to play professional basketball – sent good wishes to others and blessed the lake. I watched him carefully put his boat on the lake and let it go.

Daddy held his little sailboat tightly. I could see he didn't want to send it off. "Come on Dad, just let it go," I said to encourage him. He just couldn't. I guess sometimes you need to be ready.

By now, Aunty Miri and Uncle Dan were happier. Aunty Miri, who was dating again, began to understand that the butterfly-in-your- stomach feeling of love eventually goes away and what's important is choosing to be kind and generous in a relationship. Sharing love was like letting her Pixie Dixie boat go for someone else to find and enjoy. She had come to realize that finding her true love – and loving him despite his quirks – would occur in its own time, just like finding her Pixie Dixie boat in the secret tree.

Uncle Dan called and let us know that a couple weeks after the failed launch of his Pixie Dixie, he tried again – successfully. His Pixie Dixie now was on its journey in the big Atlantic. He felt calmer, was dealing with life's ups and downs, and was spending more time with his children.

CHAPTER EIGHT

A Blessing

THE LAST WEEKEND before school, my family and I walked up to the bridge from our lake to the next one. Mom was holding her boat tight; I wasn't sure she'd be able to let go. But she passed her boat around to all of us for extra wishes on it, closed her eyes, blessed the lake, took a really long, deep breath and dropped her Pixie Dixie from the bridge. The current carried it away, toward the next lake.

We walked back to the ice cream shop window by my favorite tree next to the lake. There, we saw Grandpa waiting for us, eating a banana, and Grandma eating an ice cream cone. "We'll be right back Grandpa and Grandma!" I said, noticing someone at the dock.

It was our boatman, Captain Mark, holding the rope of a real sailboat! Mark wore a cowboy hat with three feathers in the brim. His cheeks were bright pink. A black canvas bag labeled Pixie Dixie was cozily tucked on the sailboat bench next to him. He motioned for us to join him and we all squeezed onto the sailboat – one that doesn't fit in the palm of your hand. As we left the dock, the warm breeze pushed the sail and we began to drift out across the big lake.

It was a lovely afternoon of sailing. Mom was feeling more capable and had found a job she loved, and she had written a story that touched her heart. Mom opened her backpack and took out...

A PEANUT BUTTER, JELLY AND CUCUMBER SANDWICH for Captain Mark.

I dug down into Mom's backpack. I felt a fuzzy little feather. I reached a little deeper and pulled out a little sailboat with a pink feather as the sail – one Mom and I had made, modeling it after Mark's Pixie Dixies. On the tiny Pixie Dixie's boat's deck, we had engraved: "Thank you boatman for being a blessing. Good Luck!" I gently placed our little boat in the palm of our boatman's hand. "Thank you for teaching us how to let go," Mom said, smiling with tears in her eyes. I gave our boatman a big hug, and said: "We have everything we need!"

1. What did the characters in the story learn?

2. What would you do with your own Pixie Dixie?

3. What would your Pixie Dixie look like?

4. If you let a Pixie Dixie go, where would you let it go?

5. Do you want to make a boat?

6. What would you need to make a boat?

7. What things are holding you back?

8. Which things would you let go of?

9. Who are the people in your life that make a difference?

10. What do you need in your life?

11. What do you want in your life?

12. Is there something else besides a PIXIE DIXIE that you would make to give to others?

13. What positive things make you happy?

14. For what are you grateful?

SUPPLIES
chunk of tree bark found on the ground or in the water • pen or sharp tool for carving (adult supervision recommended) • 2 sharp flat stones • feather(s)

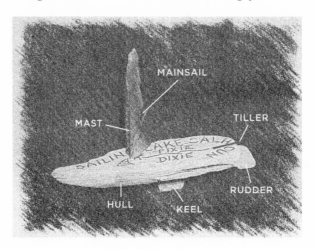

INSTRUCTIONS

1. Find a chunk of tree-bark on the walking trail around the lake or washed up on shore.

2. Carve, sand down and shape the wood to be the body of the tiny boat. Or rub the wood against the sidewalk to get the desired shape.

3. Wedge a sharp rock vertically at the stern *(back end of the boat, like a rudder)*.

4. Find the center of balance and put another sharp flat rock in the middle of the boat, sticking down as the keel – the centerline of the boat's bottom.

5. Find a feather for the sail and poke a tiny hole that will hold the feather snugly.

6. Place feather into the hole making sure it has a tight fit.

7. Wash hands thoroughly after touching feathers.

8. Add your design and signature.

9. Hold onto your boat or Set it free and Let Go!

journal

My Hopes

_____

_____

_____

_____

_____

_____

_____

My Good Wishes to Others

_____

_____

_____

_____

_____

_____

_____

My Blessing for the Lake

_____

_____

_____

_____

_____

_____

_____

in memory of (great) Grandma Tania

MY GRANDMA TANIA, who died at age 93, was a strong and capable woman. She worked hard as an architect in a time when women seldom had professional jobs. She is the reason we are alive and here today! In 1941, as German bombs were falling on her city of Babrusk, Belarus, she and her small daughter Clava, my mother, were saved only because Grandma Tania knew the captain of a ship taking refugees to safety. He recognized her standing on the dock waving and he turned the ship around to pick them up. The ship captain risked the lives of 300 passengers to save them. It was a miracle that they were saved. She left almost everything behind. Mom always says: "When you let things go, good things come back to you, especially if you are grateful for what you have."

NEAL GENDLER, EDITOR
In celebration of mother
CERNA MARTIN GENDLER | 100th Birthday on May 17, 2014

JOAN FRENZ, GRAPHIC DESIGNER
In memory of her sister
TRACY LYNN McCARRELL | May 17, 1970-August 11, 1999

A WISE MAN once told me to surround myself with amazing people, which I have done. To those I have met, who have supported me in my personal life and in my work, thank you. You have brought love into my life. Thank you in advance to those I will meet; I look forward to surrounding myself with more amazing people. I am truly blessed.

–

Made in the USA
San Bernardino, CA
25 October 2014